DISCOVERING
MY
KINGDOM
CALLING

George S. Savins

DISCOVERING MY KINGDOM CALLING

XULON PRESS ELITE

Xulon Press Elite
2301 Lucien Way #415
Maitland, FL 32751
407.339.4217
www.xulonpress.com

Paperback ISBN-13: 978-1-6628-2300-8
Ebook ISBN-13: 978-1-6628-2301-5

TABLE OF CONTENTS

Chapter 1

CALLING

---

noun
call·ing | \ ˈkȯ-liŋ \
Definition of *calling*.

1: a strong inner impulse toward a particular course
of action especially when accompanied by convic-
tion of divine influence.[1]

Whenever I think of the calling to be a pastor, evan-
gelist, teacher, I think of my pastor, Pastor Glen,
as he was called into the ministry. Ever heard that said
before? They are the ones that had a "call "on their lives
early, went to seminary, seem to have it all together, and

have it all figured out. Sound familiar? I don't think I really understood the word "calling," or maybe was not interested in what that word had to do with me. After all, I never heard the voice, or got the call, for the call.

My life as a Christian, as a disciple, really hasn't been long. I came to Christ late in life (February 2005) when I was fifty-one years old. I watched my wife Wendy take our four kids to church week after week, kept them involved in children's ministry, and watched her write a check monthly to the church for tithing. She would ask me if I wanted to come to church, but I always had other stuff to do. I have been self-employed since June of 1987 with my company, Savins Landscapes. We design, install, and maintain landscapes, both commercial and residential. I love what I do, getting up early and working outside in the elements to transform the ordinary to the extra-ordinary. I am still actively involved daily with my company.

When I did get saved, repented of my sins, asked Jesus to forgive me of my sins, and let Him become Lord of my life, I tried to prove to God that I was a different person. I will detail all that with you in chapter 7.

I have had two mentors in my life. Pastor Bill Watson was my first pastor who shared the gospel with me sixteen years ago, teaching me the biblical principles and promises of God. He always told me I was important to God and gave me my first two "Christian books": *The Knowledge of the Holy* by A.W. Tozer and *Systematic Theology* by Wayne Gruden. I read both books yearly, as they were foundational in my walk. I do not talk with Bill often, but when I do, he is always there with the godly wisdom I need. He's a true man of God that has an unbelievable testimony!

The second is John Hardimon. I met John five days after I had been saved. He was the first of many for me: my first Bible teacher; my first worship leader; my first to get a team involved in kingdom-minded work; first to work outside the four walls of the church; my first small group teacher; first to get me involved in worldwide missions (Here's Life Africa – HLA) ; and the first with the Master's Program . This was a program that shows Christian leaders and marketplace leaders how to change their world while expanding God's kingdom. Both men are younger than me, and I am eternally grateful for their willingness to disciple and mentor me.

I got saved, started reading my Bible, stopped all my hobbies (stupid and legalistic), started tithing, was asked to lead a men's group, asked to be the men's pastor, played bass on worship teams, was asked to be the executive pastor under my pastor, asked to train and put into systems for all on staff and leadership positions, taught (and still teach) a Sunday School class, and became a chaplain. I am not on staff currently, but still get to teach a small group. I was a server at my church, supporting it with our tithes and offerings, and made myself available so my giftings could be used ... in a biblical way, wouldn't you say? Not bad for a kid who grew up in Oak Cliff, a southern section of Dallas, Texas, got kicked out of Texas A & M the third week I was there, and never went to seminary school.

Is that what being a good Christian is about? is that what Jesus meant by being a disciple? Is that all there is to being set apart, holy, a kingdom- minded person? NO. Don't get me wrong: What church wouldn't love to have members do what I did, serve, give, and teach, all with a cheerful spirit?

But that is not what and why you were created.

Chapter 2

GOD'S DIVINE INVOLVEMENT AND PLAN FOR YOUR CALLING

D id you realize that God was involved in every aspect of your creation; I mean, down to the smallest detail? We are going to systematically look at what the Bible says about God and your life. Let us take my personality out of the equation and look at the TRUTH of the matter. You know the good thing about knowing the "truth"? The next time your wife says something about what you did or are doing, you can say, "Honey, do not be mad at me. Talk to God; He created me this way," and then just walk away!

Look with me in Genesis chapter 1, verses 26-27; **Then God said, "Let US make man in OUR image, according to our likeness..." So, God created man in His own image; in the image of God, He created him; male and female He created them.**

So, we see from the creation story that the Trinity, "US," is in complete agreement, as mankind is created from their decision. The Bible says we are created in His image and here is what that means. The word "attribute," the ways of God, or the way God is, is implied in that word. This is where we see some of the same attributes and characteristics that we possess, and that God possesses also. These are called communicable attributes, or commonly called similar attributes. So, let's define attributes.

God is good, and man can be good also. God is merciful; man can give mercy. God is a provider; man provides also. You can see the commonality here, so as God created us, He wanted us to be image- bearers of Him. That's why we possess certain "godly qualities" and also verifies the statement that we are "like" Him because we were created in His likeness. When we are good to our neighbors, we are like God. When we love our wives, we are displaying God's love. See how it works? It seems elementary but extremely important, once all the parts are in place and you know what to do with them.

God also possess incommunicable attributes, which are attributes that only God can possess; therefore, when we say He is transcendent, God is above everything, He is not ordinary.

God is infinite, while we are mortal; we had a beginning and will have an end, while God has neither. God is omnipresence and is everywhere at the same time, while we are only present in the now. Another illustration would be to say that God is omnipotent, where He knows everything; we can only know some things.

Look at Genesis 2:7: **And the Lord formed man of the dust of the ground and breathed into his nostrils the breath of life; and man became a living creature.** The Lord formed man. In the original language of Hebrew, according to Strong's Exhaustive Concordance of the Bible, the meaning of "formed," (3335) yatsar, a prime root; to press into shape, to mold, to determine, to fashion, to frame for a purpose.[2] Are you kidding me ...? No, I am not kidding you. Have you ever thought about you as a being from God's perspective? There is nothing missing in you, as He is involved in all aspects of your creation; and He did it for a PURPOSE.

I picture God leaning down to man's level, holding him close to Himself, and looking into his eyes as He breathes the breath of life into his nostrils. "Awake, my son; you are perfectly created. I have given you a life of abundance and have given purpose to your being. Yes, my son (mankind), you have a purpose in My kingdom." Look at God's original plan and purpose for mankind, found in the second part of **chapter 1:26 in Genesis (NKJV).**

"Let them have dominion over the fish of the sea, over the birds of the air, over the cattle, over ALL the earth, and over every creeping thing that creeps on the earth." Yes, that is right. You can read it right here in the beginning of mankind's life. God made us in His image for a purpose, a kingdom calling. What was it? It was to have dominion over the entire earth. What does that mean, to have dominion? The Strong's Concordance defines the word this way, in the original Hebrew language, (7287) radah; a prime root, to tread down, to subjugate, to have control of, to prevail against, to reign.[3]

In the creation story, we see the hand of God speaks everything into existence. God owns everything, and it is His to do as He pleases. He answers to no one, takes advice from no one, or consults with anyone, but why? Because He is God Almighty and has made everything. Now that we have established this, where does mankind fit into His creation story? I believe at the very beginning of time; you see two principles being initiated; the first being the principle of stewardship. God owns everything, BUT He created us to "steward," which involves having the authority (dominion) to take care of all for God.

The second principle is the treasure principle. The Garden of Eden was a treasure: It was valuable and full of wonderous things, and God created mankind to be His stewards to maintain it and make it fruitful. We will discuss in more detail these two principles in the next chapter.

Look at Exodus, chapter 4 vs. 11 (NKJV): **So the Lord said to him (Moses) "Who has made man's mouth? Or who makes the mute, the deaf, the seeing or the blind? Have not I, the Lord?"** So, let me put the text into proper context for you. Moses had been a shepherd for forty years. He approaches the mountain of the Lord, Mt. Horeb, where he hears the voice of the Lord and sees the burning bush that does get consumed by fire. He receives his kingdom calling, assignment, which is to,

"Go let My people free so they can worship Me"(Exod. 5:1, NKJV). What does Moses do? He starts telling God, "Hey, look here, you do not want to send me. I am a nobody. If I go, what do I do if they ask me what Your name is?" God replies, "I AM WHO I AM."

He makes another excuse, saying, "You cannot send me. I am slow of speech" (Exod. 4:10, NKJV). I guess he stutters or gets his words mixed up, but that is where God has had enough, and we have this recorded for us in verse 11. God tells us He is the one who determines who the blind is, who the mute is, who the deaf is. God is involved in everybody's formation, even those with defects. There are no accidents or blatant sins of the parents (as was the thinking in biblical times). No, it is God the Creator who decides the quality of life we all start with. Each person is perfectly formed.

Our next stop is the book of Jeremiah, chapter 29 vs. 11-13. Here is the context: It is 597 BC. The Israelites are being taken into captivity, while some have been in captivity, when God speaks these truths about His children. V. 13: **For I know the plans that I have towards you, says the Lord, they are plans of good and not for disaster, to give you a future and a hope.** God thinks about you and me, because we are special to Him. He cares about our wellbeing and has plans for us (your kingdom calling \ assignment). The plans are good, not evil or disastrous. The plans will give you hope and a future. Vs. 14: **In those days when you pray, I will listen.** When you see the phrase, "I will listen," it means that God hears your cry and immediately starts working on His plan to answer you. His hand starts moving, and He does not wait. **"If you look for me wholeheartedly, you will find me" (Jeremiah 29:12, NLT).** But we are to seek Him, not casually, but with intentionality, with fervor, and with persistence.

One more place to see God's hand involved in the formation of mankind is shown in the beautiful Psalm 139:13, written by King David (NKJV).

Vs.13: **For you formed my inward parts; You covered me in my mother's womb.**

I will praise You, for I am wonderfully made; Marvelous are your works, and my soul knows them very well. my frame was not hidden from You, when I was

made in secret, and skillfully wrought in the lowest parts of the earth.

Your eyes saw my substance being yet unformed. and in your book, they were all written, the days fashioned for me, when yet there were none of them.

What a great illustration of God's involvement in each one of our lives. God is the one who formed all parts of you, externally and internally, and because of that, we should praise God continually. Why? Is He not perfect? Well, He perfectly formed you. There are no imperfections in you. The psalmist goes on to say that He created you marvelously and the innermost part of you, your soul, knows that. It was in secret when God formed us, but now that you are created, you are God's workmanship and should be displayed in front of the entire world!

So, the truth, as recorded in the Bible, shows you were no accident. You are lacking nothing in your kingdom calling, and no one is able or supposed to do your calling. You are unique in all aspects of your being. Start searching for your kingdom calling so God will reveal to you what that assignment is for you.

Chapter 3

WHO ARE YOU AND WHY WERE YOU CREATED?

The apostle Paul is in prison under house arrest; it is around 60-62 AD (Acts 28:16-31) and he is writing a letter to the church at Ephesus, which he founded on his third missionary journey (Acts 19). He pastored the church for about three years and then turned it over to his apprentice Timothy, who continued to lead the church. Paul is now writing to the church to warn them of false teachers who are trying to penetrate the body and add things to the gift of salvation, encouraging the body as they stay committed to Jesus.

I love chapter 1 of Ephesians, the first fourteen verses. If you ever feel afraid; if you have anxiety; if you are unsure of who you are; if you feel neglected, abused, or just not worth anything, read Ephesians chapter 1: 1-14. These verses tell you who you really are.

Blessed (vs.3)
Chosen (vs. 4)
Predestined (vs. 5)
Adopted (vs. 5)
Accepted (vs. 6)
Redeemed (vs. 7)
Forgiven (vs. 7)
Enlightened (vs. 8,9)
Given an inheritance (vs. 11)
Sealed (vs. 13)
Assured (vs. 14)

Let us spend a few moments examining each of these.

We are blessed.

Blessed
bless·ed
/blest, 'blesid/
adjective

1. made holy; consecrated.[4]

Blessed means you have the favor of God upon you, with you, and on you. It also says, "with ALL," there are no blessings that are not yours. ALL of them are available to you, and God is bestowing them on you.

Chosen

Chosen

/'CHōzən/

Verb

1. past participle of **choose.**

Adjective

1. having been selected as the best or most appropriate person.[5]

Before the foundation of the world, before creation when it was just the Father, the Son, and the Holy Spirit surrounded by "nothingness," they decided unanimously that you would be chosen to be a follower of Christ. Of all the people God formed, you were chosen for a specific plan.

Predestined
predestined
/prēˈdestind/
adjective

1. (of an outcome or course of events) determined in advance by divine will or fate.[6]

God, in advance of anything that you have done, said, or thought, knew you so well and felt was so important to Him that He predestined you to greatness. You like apples, how 'bout them apples!!

Adopted
a·dopt
/əˈdäpt/
verb
past tense: **adopted**; past participle: **adopted**.

1. legally take (another's child) and bring it up as one's own.[7]

God has decided to take you away from Satan's grasps and raise you as His own son\ daughter. That comes with all the benefits, provisions, wisdom, and the direction from the creator of the universe.

Accepted

accepted

/kept/

adjective

1. generally believed or recognized to be valid or correct.[8]

God has validated you as His chosen one, recognizing you as being capable and worthy to do His will, accomplishing mighty eternal works in His Kingdom. This means that you always have access to Him, and there is nothing you can do that keeps you from being accepted by Him. Nothing, remember that!

Redeemed

redeem

/rəˈdēm/

verb

past tense: **redeemed**; past participle: **redeemed.**

1. to compensate for the faults or bad aspects of (something).[9]

God has justified you in His sight because He sees you as He sees His son: pure, holy, without blemish. Because when Jesus went to the cross, He shed His blood for your sins. His blood covered you, so God see you as a redeemed, or new, person, a new creation.

Forgiven

for·give·ness

/ˌfərˈgivnəs/

noun

Psychologists generally **define forgiveness** as a conscious, deliberate decision to release feelings of resentment or vengeance toward a person or group who has harmed you, regardless of whether they deserve your **forgiveness**.[10]

All your sins (past, present, and future) are forgiven. Not only that but the Bible says God is ready to forgive you, waiting patiently for you to ask for forgiveness. Psalm 88:5 says, **"For Lord you are good and ready to forgive, and abundant in mercy for all those who call upon You."** Remember:

You are pure in God's eyes. There is nothing that separates you from Him once you have repented of your sins.

Enlightened

en·light·ened

/in'lītnd, en'lītnd/

adjective

1. having or showing a rational, modern, and
    well-informed outlook.
    give (someone) greater knowledge and under-
    standing about a subject or situation.[11]

God has, and will, enlighten you, giving you the advice, instruction, and guidance in all your works until those works, assignments, are finished. When God starts something with you, it will be finished ... completely.

Given an inheritance.

Inheritance
in·her·it·ance
/inˈherədəns/
noun
noun: **inheritance**; plural noun: **inheritances**

1. a thing that is inherited. The passing on of spiritual and earthly gifts that God passes on to His children.[12]

Since we are part of a family, God's family, we are entitled to an inheritance, all that God owns, which is "everything" now available to you, His son or daughter. When we ask for things, I think we forget who we are talking to, who our real Father is: The almighty, omnipresence, infinite God of the universe.

Sealed

seal[1]

/ˈsē(ə)l/

verb

past tense: **sealed**; past participle: **sealed**.

1. fasten or close securely.
   conclude, establish, or secure (something)
   definitively, excluding the possibility of
   reversal or loss.[13]

We have been sealed with the Word of truth, the gospel of our salvation, when we believed God and are promised the Holy Spirit. It means that we can never be taken away from God: no event, circumstance, situation removes us from God. The Holy Spirit "seals" us with an identifying mark that is on us. So, when God looks down from heaven, He sees the mark of each of us, identifying us as one of His children. He never loses track of us; He is always aware of our whereabouts and is proud of each of us.

Assured

assured

/ə'SHo͝ord/

adjective

adjective: **assured**.

1. confident.
2. protected against discontinuance or change.
3. tell someone something positively or confidently to dispel any doubts they may have.[14]

Finally, we have been assured or guaranteed by the indwelling of the Holy Spirit that who we are is we are now complete and ready for the why. Why has God done all this for us?

Remember back in chapter 1, I told you I loved systematic theology. It just makes sense to me. It is logical; it is in order. God explains to us who we are in Him because He has a plan for our lives ...it is our kingdom callings or kingdom assignments. In Ephesians chapter 2, He starts to give us revelation on why chapter 1 comes before chapter 2. He has now made us alive, who were once dead in our sins (v1). We used to walk with the prince of power of the air (Satan), whose spirit is with the sons of disobedience (v2). Remember that we once walked in this darkness (v3):

> **BUT GOD who is rich in mercy, because of His great love which He loved us even when we were dead in trespasses, made us alive together with Christ (by grace you have been saved), and raised us up together in the heavenly places in Christ Jesus, that in the ages to come He might show the exceeding riches of His grace in His kindness towards us in Christ Jesus. For by grace, you have been saved through faith and not of yourself, it is a gift from God, not of works, lest anybody should boast. For we are His workmanship, created in Christ Jesus for good works** (your kingdom calling or your kingdom assignment) **which God prepared beforehand that we should walk in them.**

Before the creation of the world, God divinely created you, knitted you, put you together, formed every part of you, put you in the time period you were born, and gave you parents. He blessed you, chose you, predestined you, adopted you, accepted you, redeemed you, forgave you, enlightened you, gave you an inheritance, sealed you with the power and the mark of the Holy Spirit, and then guarantees you that the "good work" (i.e., your kingdom assignment) will produce a hundred times the fruit, have earthly and eternal consequences, and will give you eternal rewards that will take an eternity to see.

Are you kidding me? ...No, I am not!!

Here is the rest of the story from Ephesians chapter 1. The word workmanship in Ephesians 2:10 is the Greek word poema. We get the word poem from the literal translation. What God is trying to illustrate is that you are a "masterpiece." Think about where masterpieces are located. The great works of past artists are on display so all can see, appreciate, and be inspired ... that is why God created you. You are His masterpiece, so all can see, admire, and be inspired to be like you. What does this do ...it brings glory to God. The sole purpose of mankind is to point all to Jesus, so our Father can be glorified.

Do you see it? God uses ordinary people (you and I) to redeem them and do everything from Ephesians chapter 1:1-14, and then lets us work in His kingdom. He creates us uniquely for a kingdom calling\ assignment that no one else can do, only you. Think about that; to me, that is the most humbling thing I have ever heard of, especially when you see my past that I will share in chapter 7. One more thing: The work He has created for us says it's "good work." Of course, it is. God is good; everything He does is good, so the works/assignment He has for us has to be good.

I believe one day when we have our glorified bodies and Jesus and I are out by ourselves in His garden (that I probably will be working in it since I am a gardener), we will be talking about my calling, my assignment. I will say something like, "You know, Jesus, that was so much fun. I never got bored; it really was so easy. It was effortless when I was working in my assignment." And Jesus will look at me and say, "Oh Georgie (like my dad used to), of course you enjoyed it. Of course, it produced a hundred times the fruit. It is what I created you for."

Chapter 4

THE TREASURE AND YOUR CALLING

The treasure and your calling, what are they all about? Why is it important to understand this principle, and how it is foundational to working out your kingdom calling \ assignment? I was first introduced to a book called *The Treasure Principle* by Randy Alcorn by my good friend Andy Blakesly. He is the president of Here's Life Africa, based here locally in the DFW area, specifically in Plano, Texas at the Hope Center. We were going through this small book together. He was leading me through the principles, then I was to find another guy and take him through the principles. *The Treasure Principle* is a book that when you start to put into practice the principles, it will transform your life. You will start thinking kingdom eternity, not kingdom earthly. He talks about "principal keys" as he unlocks God's Word. I highly recommend you pick up the book and start to put into practice the keys, and then share them with someone ese. It will help keep you focused on kingdom things. The keys are listed in each chapter of *The Treasure Principle*.

In the Sermon on the Mount, Jesus says this in Matthew 6:19—21 (NLT):

> **Do not store up treasures here on earth, where months eat them and rust destroys them, and where thieves break in and steal. Store our treasures in heaven, where moths and rust cannot destroy, and thieves do not break in and steal. Wherever your treasure is, there the desires of your heart will also be.**

So, let us set up the Scripture's context so we can accurately hear what God is trying to tell us, and so we can put the information into the proper application mode. This is Jesus's first sermon. The multitudes are present; the religious leaders are present, as well as the disciples. Jesus is introducing us to His "new" kingdom, a kingdom that requires a repentance (changed heart) and where values come from the inside, not the outside. Jesus is trying to illustrate to us what the new kingdom people will look like, how they will think, and where their priorities should be. That is the context.

First, let us define what some of the earthly treasures are: cars, houses, boats, clothing, jewelry, hobbies, and things that we put value on and identify as who we are. In context, there is nothing wrong with any of these "things" ...but our lives cannot be consumed in having them, in pursuing them, and in being obsessed with them. There has to be more to life than possessions. After all, when you die, you cannot take them with you, right?

He does not say we shouldn't have treasures (things that are valuable, important). He said that earthly treasures have no real lasting value: they are eaten; they rust; people steal them. But in heaven, your treasures have eternal value. They have eternal importance, so the conclusion He draws is to go after treasures, but just be sure they are kingdom treasures.

Jesus says, "Wherever your treasure is, there the desires of your heart will also be." Luke 19:10 says (NKJV),

"Jesus came to seek and save that which is lost." That was Jesus's kingdom calling\ assignment ... leave the glory of heaven, go to earth as a baby, born in a manger, grew up in poverty, was persecuted, beaten, willingly die (for me and you), and then raised by the Father on the third day. What does that mean in the context of the Treasure Principle? If people's salvation was important to Jesus, and it is, shouldn't people's salvation be important to us? When people get saved, their homes are in heaven now. They must wait a little while to occupy those homes, but they are there. People are treasures to God.

You see, Jesus was focused on the lost. In Christian lingo, we will say something like, "They have a PASSION for the lost." Jesus was passionate about the lost. He was passionate about them, so nothing was more important than spreading the gospel: no length of day, with food or without food, being accepted in a region or being chased out. He was so passionate He died for the lost ... now that's passion.

You too will find your focus, your passion, your kingdom calling. God has already created it for you (Ephesians 2:10: good works). It will be like being on a treasure hunt, and when you find the treasure, it will be the most important thing in your life. Eternally speaking, it will be rewarding, as you will be fulfilled because you will be complete. Remember, the first assignment God gave mankind was to work (be a steward) in His garden. God created man to work, to accomplish good works, your kingdom calling.

Just to bring home the point, to bring the whole council of God together, let us look at these parallel Scriptures. Go with me to Luke chapter 15, the parables of the" lost" and their importance to Jesus as He works out His kingdom calling.

Jesus is ministering to society's outcasts: they are the tax collectors, sinners, probably Gentiles, and Jews who were not following the Law. This was totally out of character. Jesus claimed to be from God, was God's son, but the Pharisees and religious taught and believed that God hated sinners and would cast judgement on them at any moment. In fact, they believed judgment had already fallen on them. But Jesus was freely hanging out with the outcasts. Why? Because He loved them. They had value to Him. To say it again, they were valuable to God. You are valuable to God.

The first parable Jesus shares with the outcasts has to do with losing a sheep, Luke 15 vs.4-7. The shepherd, we are told, has a hundred sheep and one of them goes missing. I mean it is only one; there are still ninety-nine left. In the cost of doing business, sometimes there are losses, right? The owner in this parable is God. We are the sheep, and we wander, don't we? We think things are better in the next pasture: greener, lusher, less work involved. But that is not what happens. God sees the one lost sheep as valuable, so valuable that He leaves the ninety-nine and goes and does not stop until He finds the sheep and carries it home. You see the compassion, love, and care of God. There is no anger displayed at all, as God is focused on that one, lost sheep. God is passionate about that one lost person. Why? He was called to seek and find the lost.

In the second parable, a woman has ten silver coins (probably from her marriage ceremony), and while cleaning her house, she loses one. Just to be in context here, the floor was dirt, probably with some fodder, or some type of native grass that had been put on the dirt floor to keep the house less dusty, to have some semblance of neatness to it. She would have to meticulously go through every piece, strand of grass, to find the coin, working tirelessly until she found it ... you see, the coin has value to her.

So, from God's perspective, even though there are still nine coins left, the one that is missing has value to Him. Jesus came so that none would perish. You see the focus again for the lost; we see God's passion on display for us ... remember we are to be image-bearers. We will discover what our focus should be, as it will be a passion that allows us to expand God's kingdom. It will become our calling; it will become our kingdom assignment that allows us to use all our spiritual giftings and earthly talents to find and deposit treasures in heaven that have eternal value.

Finally, let us look at the third parable, probably the most famous of all, The Prodigal Son. It is found in Luke 15: vs. 11-32. We all know the story, so I am going to look at the parable through the father's eyes (the father represents God).

The father had two sons; the younger wants to be on his own, asks for his inheritance (a great "cultural insult"), and leaves the father. He spends all the money, lives like an animal, comes to his senses, and wants to come back to his father's house, not as his son but as one of His slaves.

Vs. 18: "I will arise and go to my father and will say to him, 'Father I have sinned against heaven and before you, and I am no longer worthy to be called your son. make me like one of your hired servants.'"

The son is right about one thing: he, in himself, is not worthy to be the father's son anymore, that is for sure. But when the son confesses, all the son's sins are instantly forgiven, wiped clean, and no longer seen by the father. The father sees His son restored, forgiven, and now justified to be at His side ... the son (you and I) is valuable, important, special, and useful to God. The restoration is immediate; there is no period of going to "time out" for punishment; to reflect on your bad decisions; to earn your way back to sonship. No, that's not what God does: He waits for us (v20); He runs after us (v20b); He kisses us (act of love kindness) (v20c). The father has "the best robe" put on the son (v22a). The son is again recognized by all around that He is truly the son; that all privileges and prestige are now with the son again. The ring is put back on his finger (v22b). He has all the authority as the father has and has the sandals put on his feet. Slaves did not wear sandals, but the son does. The final step in the son's restoration is the father, Father God, acts this way every single time someone comes to Him or comes back to Him.

Then the father shows all the kingdom the importance by slaughtering the fatted calf and celebrating with all who are present, sons and slaves. The only one not there is the older son, which again we see God taking the lead and going to the other son to explain He was right to celebrate ... the son was once dead, but now is alive. The older son represents the religious leaders of the time. They just could not understand the love of the Father; they thought it was all about do's and don'ts. But you see, it is more than that; it is about a relationship with Jesus. The Bible says that He loved us so much that while we were still sinners, He gave his life for us (Rom. 5:8).

That is being passionate. Jesus sees us as treasures, and His call was to come and get us. What is your calling? What are you going to be focused on? What is going to be your passion?

Chapter 5

UNDERSTANDING THE DIFFERENCE BETWEEN OWNERSHIP AND STEWARDSHIP

As a disciple, as a kingdom-minded person, it is helpful for me to review the basics. Remember how it was in the beginning of your salvation; you could not wait to get up and start to pray. You shared everything with God, the "big "and the "small." Why? Because that's what the Bible says to do. You would write the tithe check and tell Him, "Check it out, Father. We really did good this month ...thanks for all Your help." Your preparation for your Sunday school was filled with God's truth, and you could not wait to share all you had learned that week with each of them.

I once heard Troy Aikman, three-time Super Bowl-winning quarterback, Hall of Famer talk about those winning years during a national broadcast of an NFL game. He would say it all starts in the off season, where he and his center would practice snapping the ball before training camp even started. Why? If Troy doesn't get the snap, there is no pass to Irvin in the end zone.

The basics are important. Here is a basic Bible principle: God owns everything, we are just His stewards. What does this mean?

We hear it all the time. I finally paid off my truck, I own it now; or you paid off your house, it is yours, finally, after thirty years, yea!! Here is what the Bible says about God and His ownership:

First Corinthians 6:19-29: **You are not your own: you were bought with a price.**

Haggai 2:8: **"The silver is mine and the gold is mine," declares the Lord Almighty.**

Psalm 24:1: **The earth is the Lord's and everything in it, the world and all who live in it.**

Deuteronomy 8:18: **Remember the Lord your God, for it is he who gives you the ability to produce wealth.**

Four scriptures spanning thousands of years, all saying the same thing … God owns everything.

Ownership

own·er·ship
/'ōnər͵SHip/
noun

1. the act, state, or right of possessing something.[15]

A straightforward definition. Since God created everything, He possesses it. He can do with it as He likes. He owns it, including our lives. Can there be two owners of the same thing? No, not really. So, if God is the sole owner of our lives, our possessions, what are our roles? What are we supposed to do?

The answer is we are God's stewards, caretakers of all.

Stewardship

stew·ard·ship

/ˈst(y)ōōərdˌSHip/

noun

1. the job of supervising or taking care of something, such as an organization or property.[16]

So, according to the definition above, we have a job, a calling, an assignment to look after ALL God has given us. This also implies that at one time or another, we will have to give an account on how well we took care of all that God has given us ... ever thought about that?

Here is an illustration from the Bible: The unjust steward (Lk. 16:1-13).

Here is the context of the story. A wealthy master (God) has a steward (mankind) that God has entrusted with taking care of all his possessions. An accusation comes to the master that the steward has been stealing from him. Here is what happens. The steward manipulates (changes) the books so it looks like the losses are smaller than they really are, hoping that after he gets fired, the people who he changed their accounts might let him stay with them, because he is too old to dig for work and does not want to beg.

Here is the application: We are stewards for God. He chooses us and assigns each of us something to do in His kingdom. He will always find out what we have done in His absence, and we will be held accountable for what we did or did not do with God's assignment for us. Make no mistake: If you are not actively working in His kingdom, you have got serious problems when you stand before Him. In verse 10, God says **this: "He who is faithful in what is least is faithful also in much, and he who is unjust in what is least, is unjust in much."**

Life is a test. That is what God does with His children; He has always done that with us. He tested us in the garden, but we failed. He tested the children in the wilderness; they failed, so He kept them there forty years. And He will test us. Will you pass the test? All is His, so be mindful of whatever He gives you to work with.

To give us another illustration from the Bible, look at Matthew 25: 14 – 30. Jesus tells us what the Kingdom of Heaven is like.

A man traveling to a far country: the man is God, the far country is the territory God has placed you in. God has servants (stewards) whom He gives a certain amount of money to (talents {in the NT, it represented the value of a coin or money}). Five, two, one were given to the three servants. Verse 19: **"After a long time the lord of those servants came and settled accounts with each of them."**

Their servants have died, are standing before God, and God is going over their assignments with each of them.

"What did you do with your assignment, your kingdom calling?"

Each of them reported. Some produced a great amount of fruit, and some smaller amounts of fruit, but they were each rewarded.

They had new assignments in the eternal kingdom. They will be ruling and exercising authority over cities that have people. You can figure it out.

Except for the one who had a calling, an assignment, one that was chosen, blessed, pre-destined, redeemed, well you get the picture: and he did nothing with His calling.

His one talent is taken from him and given to the one with the most, five.

Verse 29 says, **"For to everyone who has, more will be given, and he will have an abundance, but from him who does not have, even what he has will be taken away."** What happened to the third servant? Verse 30: **"And cast the unprofitable servant into the outer darkness? There will be weeping and gnashing of teeth."** Not my words, but Jesus's words.

Could it be that being a Christian, a disciple, is more than going to church, sitting in a pew, helping put the chairs up, greeting people, or making coffee for the members? Is God's expectations more than that? Is that why He spent so much time knitting you together, forming you, choosing you, etc.? Is that the "good works" He is talking about in Ephesians 2:10? Is that really your kingdom calling?

Chapter 6

The Three P's (Purpose, Passion, Potential)

The three P's.

God's Kingdom Purpose.
Your God-honored Passion,
Your God–Designed Potential

Purpose
pur·pose
/ˈpərpəs/
noun

1. the reason for which something is done or created
    or for which something exists.[17]

Have you ever thought about God's kingdom purpose? Here are the two key pronouncements of the Lord that represent His kingdom purpose.

The Great Commandment: Matthew 22:34-40:

> **But when the Pharisees heard that He silenced the Sadducees, they gathered. Then one of them a lawyer, asked Him a question, testing Him, and saying, "Teacher, which is the greatest commandment in the law?" Jesus said to him "You shall love the Lord your God with all your heart, with all your soul, and with all your mind. This is the first and great commandment. And the second is like it 'You shall love your neighbor as yourself.' On these two commandments hang all the law and the prophets."**

Jesus is quoting two Old Testament verses. The first verse is from Deuteronomy 6:5; the second verse is from Leviticus 19:18. He is saying that the entire O T law can be summed up in these two verses. So, we see from this passage that God's kingdom was to have mankind love Him with "everything," and then to love your neighbor as you love yourself.

The Great Commission: Matthew 28: 18 -20

> **Then Jesus came and spoke to them saying, "All authority has been given to Me in heaven and on earth. Go therefore and make disciples of all the nations, baptizing them in the name of the Father, and of the Son, and of the Holy Spirit, teaching them to observe all things that I have commanded you, and lo, I am with you always, even to the end of age."**

So here is the condensed version of God's purpose to mankind: Love ME (God) with everything you have, love your neighbor as yourself, and go into all the world and make disciples. That is God's singular purpose. He was to accomplish this through His son's focus on this mission, to the point of death. That is the ultimate staying power. He was relentless, not deterred, not stopped, until that purpose was fulfilled. Why? Because you (mankind) are valuable to Him. He wanted us restored to Himself, and the only way to do it was for Jesus to shed His blood and die. That was the penalty needed to satisfy a holy, pure God. By Him dying and God being satisfied, the Father raised His son on the third day, and He now sits at the Father's right hand, a symbol of preeminence and power. His kingdom purpose was directed at joining ourselves to Him.

We (mankind) are so important that God's kingdom purpose became His honored passion. What is passion?

Passion
pas·sion
/ˈpaSHən/
noun

1.   strong and barely controllable emotion.[18]

In biblical terms, it means to suffer, to bear, to endure, it becomes an object of someone's love. We became the object of God's love. It has been that way since the beginning of the creation story. We (mankind) were the crowning creation piece for God. His creation was now complete because we were now created in His likeness, and Jesus endured and suffered even unto death because of His passion they had for us.

The first two P's are from God. God has a kingdom purpose, and it was to restore us back to Himself. The purpose became His kingdom passion. We were so much loved by the Father that His only begotten son endured and suffered for us, because we were so valuable to them. Nothing would deter Jesus, even unto death; that's how passionate He was for us. The third P is your God-designed potential. That's right; God has designed you for a kingdom potential. I call it … your kingdom calling, assignment. WE know from Ephesians 2:10 that we were created for good works; that is your kingdom calling. Now it is up to you to find your calling. It sounds scary and maybe a little too big for us, but it's not. If I can find mine, trust me, you will find yours.

Start by asking yourself what is important to you? You have been given probably multiple, spiritual gifts, certain natural talents, and have more influence over people than you realize. Seek God, ask Him, and pray, expecting an answer. That is who He is; He is waiting to unveil your calling to you. Why wouldn't He? He has set aside a hundred times the fruit for you. Your potential is only limited by your imagination and your faith in Him. Go and buy these two books, they both helped me: *The Kingdom Assignment* by Denny and Leesa Bellesi, and *Gospel Patrons* by John Rinehart. Get ready to be fulfilled and get ready to hear those words, "Well done my good and faithful servant, come and enter into the joy of YOUR Lord" (Matt. 25:21).

Chapter 7

MY STORY

The Early Years: I was born and raised in Oak Cliff; that is in the southern part of Dallas, Texas. I am the oldest of seven boys. There is me, Mike, James, Matt (Dom Belize), Richard, Tim, and Eric. Mom and Dad are gone. We were raised Catholic, and Mom would dress us all the same every week to go to Mass. I even was an altar boy at one time. We all still live in the DFW area (south of the Trinity River), except my brother Richard and me. I live in Richardson, and Richard lives in Texarkana, Texas. Mom and Dad really believed God when He said, "Be fruitful and multiply," so they did. Mike, James, Matt, Richard, and me are all one year apart, so I had a great childhood.

We moved to the Redbird area of Oak Cliff from the South Oak Cliff area when I was about thirteen. All the houses were new, but most were still under construction. We had a creek there, access to 2"x4'x8"'s and plywood. We had three tree houses built in multiple places. We had BB guns with an abundance of rabbits, squirrels, rodents, and all the sparrows you could shoot. We caught baby blue gills, thousands of craw dads with the bacon that Mom was constantly running out. We built an underground tunnel with a playroom when the movie "The Great Escape" came out. You can use your wildest imagination on what happened in there and you probably would be right on.

I was an Eagle Scout; in fact, I have a plaque in my office with a signature from then-Senator John Connolly, being at that time the youngest Eagle Scout. I think I was just fourteen. My brothers and me all went on to graduate from Bishop Dunne High School. It was awesome. You got to wear a uniform every day to school, slacks, buttoned-down shirt, a tie, and a sports coat. We looked sharp!!

The Working and Family Years: The play time was now over, and it was time for college. My dad was an Aggie, class of '47, so there was only one place the first born of the Savins was going, Texas A & M. I don't think I sent out any other "invitations" to other schools. I got accepted, Mom and Dad dropped me off, put a lot of money into a bank account for me, and said, "Don't disappoint us!!" I had shoulder-length hair at A & M, surrounded by the CORP. They were fanatics about everything: the way they dressed (sharp); the way they spoke, walked, carried their weapons; the length of their hair. They were, and still are, the real deal. I didn't see them that way back then.

Three weeks later, I was arrested, having possession of marijuana. I had to call the parents and was given two choices by the campus police: Go to jail \ prison for a long time, or don't ever attend a state college in Texas again. So, I was on my way back to Oak Cliff after my dad found a barber shop. "Cut it all off" was all he said to the barber, which he gladly did. Home again, it was awful. Dad and my brothers were mad and disappointed in me. I had let the entire family down. This was in the fall of 1971. I needed to get back on track.

A good friend of my brother's, Rick Poe, called me and asked if I wanted to help him and his dad start a burger place. I told him, "I'm in, see you in the morning." It was called Pokies, located at HWY 67 and Hampton Road. We renovated the building, bought the commercial equipment, and opened that place up. It was the forerunner to Fuddruckers, forty-five years ahead of its time. We had three sizes of burgers: quarter-pounder, half-pounder, and the Colossal burger (3\4 pounder). We would cook to order; then you would take it to the condiment station and build your own burger. I was the manager, and all was good, back on track. I kind of liked this food service industry.

We had been opened about six months when I came to work one morning to open and start the prep and noticed the building had caught fire and was destroyed, not good for me. Next door was a Pizza Inn; the GM's name was Bill Cowley. I knew him because we would occasionally switch out burgers for pizzas. I said, "Bill, I need work NOW." He said, "You're hired as a shift leader at $1.30 an hour. Be here tomorrow. Cut your hair (I had grown it out again) or get a wig." I got the wig and thus started my career with Pizza Inn.

I excelled at Pizza Inn and got promoted to my first store as a manager in Dallas at Mockingbird Lane and McMillan. It was what we called a dog store, neglected, lowest volume store in the chain. Seven months later, #1 in sales in the Dallas market. The Houston area would kick our butts weekly with their sales. They had high volume stores, and they had at least two stores that would run $1000.00 at the lunch buffet. Dallas had none, until I took over the Oak lawn store. It was Dallas's highest volume buffet store, usually around $750.00-$800.00. I took the store over and three months later, the register said $1,054.98 after the buffet was over. We finally had a Dallas store that had broken the elusive $1000.00 mark. I was promoted to area manager in the Longview area, managing the existing store. They built three more in Tyler (two), one more in Longview, and one in Magnolia, Arkansas. Now that there were five stores, I was promoted to area supervisor. Finally, my dreams were coming true.

I had met my wife Wendy in the summer of 1974; she was what we used to call "a fox," with tiny, long blonde hair down to her waist. I mean she was gorgeous! She worked at Bonanza, a steakhouse chain at the end of the block where my store at Mockingbird was located. When their shifts were over, their employees would come to my store for pizza and salad. That's when I first saw her. I knew then she was the one. So, I sent my employee, Richard (we called him "mullet"), down to Bonanza to let Wendy know I wanted a date with her. She threw him out and told him, "If he wants to go out, come down himself." Which I did; I made a fool out of myself, spilling tea all over my plate in the cafeteria line, but she finally agreed to go out. I proposed over Christmas and we were married in June of 1974.

Our first child, Laughton Christopher, was born while we were in Longview, Texas in May of 1977. In December of 1979, I was being promoted again to a regional supervisor position with seven stores in Kansas City, Missouri. Rodney Goertz, a hotshot supervisor from the Houston area, was taking the seven stores in the Kansas City, Kansas area. I was moving up, getting the house, etc. Wendy would come later; she was nine months pregnant, and Michelle Jennifer was born later in the month of December. My brother Matt came up from Dallas to be with Wendy. The stores in the Kansas City area were dog stores... they were owned by a franchise who was selling them back to the company. Long story short, I had my first failure. I never could get the stores turned around the way they needed to, so in the spring of 1982, I resigned.

I bought three Pizza Inns in the Austin area from my second supervisor, Don. My brother Richard had one of the stores, a friend of ours, Dave, had another, and I had the one across from the University of Texas on Duvall Street.

It was now the beginning of 1982 when Candace Maria was born. Shortly after that, I divorced Wendy and left her and my three children, taking a job in the "Valley," South Padre Island, Harlingen, Mc Allen with a Pizza Inn franchise named Ray Chapeaux. I would supervise the existing three stores while he built at least one more in Harlingen. Fifteen months into our arrangement, Ray suddenly died of a heart attack. The wife wanted to try and still operate as usual and continue to build the new store, but with Ray gone, we never could get the finance we needed. So, in 1984, I came back to the Dallas area, hooked up with John Tennery, who had the franchise rights to Fort Worth. He probably had about thirty or so stores. They needed a supervisor and needed to work so there I was again back in the pizza business. I stayed with the Tennery group until 1986, then went to work for another start-up hamburger place .....named Chilis.

It was the greatest place in the world to work. I was on a fast track to become GM because of all my experience in the food industry. It was a dream job. We got to wear blue jeans (mine were always lightly starched), a Ralph Lauren polo shirt (I had every color made), and dock siders. Are you kidding me? ... No, I'm not. We were Chili heads; it was a thing. We were in a class of our own, and I made GM in about nine months. The staff consisted of 85-100 food servers, 40-50 cooks, 10 or so back of the house guys, and about 10 bartenders. We were killing it every day. We were on a wait every day at lunch and on a wait Thursdays -Sundays, closed at 10:00 during the week and 11:00 on weekends. That was plenty early for us to still go out and have fun; and trust me, we did!

But I started asking Wendy to marry me again. I had really messed up doing the things I had done to her five years before. You see, we were married for seven years and had been divorced for five years. At the seven-year mark, we got re-married. Before our re-marriage, her answer was always no to reconciliation, but we did go out occasionally.

I was hopeful. The hopeful turned into reality. Wendy had gotten over the pain enough to re-marry me again. She wanted to do it on our original wedding date, so on June 5th, 1989, we were re-married. It was the second-best day of my life.

As Chili's began to expand nationally, we were bought by the Brinker group, you know him as the guy who started Steak 'n' Ale and Bennigan's. Slowly but surely, their management team crept into our stores. Their managers just didn't get it; we were now wearing slacks and white, long-sleeved shirts; horrible. They were managers, not Chili heads. Sooner than later, I clashed with one of their new supervisors. I had known him my entire time I was with Chilis, and my numbers were always better, I mean a lot better. If this was the direction we were heading, I was out. So, I left, moved back home for about thirty days when one Friday night around 6:30, I get a call from our friend Rick, "You wanna come work at a landscape company?" Absolutely. He said, "Be here Monday." I was and thus started a job that fifteen months later led me to Savins Landscapes and maintenance.

But paycheck after paycheck was bouncing, the landscape company had run out of money. I really liked this landscape stuff. I learned how to run a maintenance crew, how to read, and install a landscape plan ...I can do this. I borrowed some money from my dad, went to the Ford dealership in Mesquite on a Saturday morning during a rainstorm, had three months of bank statements with me, and became the owner of a Ford Ranger. This started the beginning of Savins Landscapes. It's now 2021 and we continue to grow and exceeds the year before in sales. We are blessed!

Salvation has come to the Savins household. It was Valentine's Day weekend, (2005). Wendy always wanted the girls with us, so my Michelli, my Candace Maria, my Sammi (Samantha Renee, our daughter after getting back together), and a couple of their girlfriends were over for a valentine's feast: smoked brisket, sausage, and all the fixings you can imagine. All of my girls and wife love to create the sides. We were getting ready to get our bellies blown up! After lunch, Wendy came up to me in front of all the girls. She said, "I don't love your father any-more, and to be honest, I don't even like him. If things don't change soon, I am going to divorce him." Are you kidding me? My Michelli and Candace Maria said, "Dad, you better get your s---- together and do it fast." I think

Samantha was in shock. I knew she was not kidding. I've been told I don't love you, but I don't even like you? I was in BIG trouble now! We had always had a marriage more like roommates than being intimate.

On the same page, I was not saved while Wendy had been saved since she was a little girl. There was always conflict over tithing, me constantly cursing, doing whatever I wanted, then apologizing, and then repeating …it really was not good. We both knew it, but I just figured we will be ok, tolerable, for a while longer.

The next weekend, it was a Saturday. I had gone to the nursery and picked out a bunch of plants because I was going to re-do our front yard. We had had new neighbors move in across the street during the previous week. The neighbor was coming over to introduce himself, but I was in no mood to talk with anyone. I was mad that things had gotten to this point. I really did love Wendy; I just was not a good person. He came over, saying, "Hi, I'm Pastor Bill Watson; just wanted to come over and say hi." I said something like, "You're not going to start telling me about Jesus, are you? You're not one of those kinds of pastors, are you?" "Do you need to do know about Jesus?" he asked. I said, "Look, my life is so f----- up right now, I can't even see straight." He told me Jesus loved me, He wanted my marriage to be fixed, and if I trusted Him, He would save me and heal my marriage. Are you kidding me? He said, "No, I'm not."

I had heard hundreds of times about Jesus from Wendy and her mother. I just was not desperate enough to believe; I was now thinking I could not lose Wendy again, no way. "What do I do?" He prayed with me, and I accepted Christ in the front yard, finished the landscape, went inside, and told Wendy I got saved, got something to eat, and went upstairs to take a shower and go to sleep.

I was now clean. I had heard somewhere about going into a secret place or closet to pray, so I went into the closet and closed the door. I was completely naked and said, "I am a deceiver. I hide things from Wendy, and I guess from You too, so here I am. I have nothing to hide. Please don't let Wendy leave." I had two hobbies at the time; one was I golfed and was really good at it. I had been playing for about seven years, shot par twice (playing from the "whites," had a documented hole in one). I dressed like Tiger Woods, even in the middle of the summer, with slacks, a Nike polo shirt with matching Nike hat, and golf shoes so polished, it made your eyes hurt to look at them. Needless to say, my buddies and family thought that I was a freak, crazy, and well, you get the gist! I would get off work, practice for hours at the putting green, and had an outstanding short game. I had a T time somewhere every Saturday and Sunday.

My other hobby was I was a fisherman, and a darn good one. I was using Ford F-150' 4x4 at this time and in the back of my truck were seven fishing poles, each one rigged with a different rig, i.e., spinner bail, plastic worm, a jig, a crank bait, a top water, a slug go, and a mepps spinner on my ultra-light. I only used Shomano bait cast, top of the line, with Berkley poles. While I was driving around, if I saw a body of water and if there were any fish in there, I would catch 'em, guaranteed. I was an expert on where to cast, what speed to retrieve, what the depth of the bait should be, etc.

Within a week of getting saved, I quit doing both. I had to show God that I was serious about this salvation stuff. So, I asked Pastor Bill what I should do. "Read your Bible and pray." So, I did what every new believer did; I started reading my Bible through three times a year. That' s right, that is not a misprint ...no one does that. It was ridiculous and legalistic at the same time. But I was showing Jesus that I was serious about getting in shape and not losing Wendy. I also started praying. The Bible says in 1 Thessalonians 5:16: **"Rejoice always, pray without ceasing, in everything give thanks, for this is the will of God in Christ Jesus for you."** If that's what the Bible says, then that's what I'll do. So, I have been rejoicing and praying without ceasing ever since.

Later in that first week that I got saved, Pastor Bill stopped by to see how I was doing. I said, "GREAT, Jesus would fix everything." I also started to brag that I play bass, and if their worship team ever needed a bass player, I would help them. He said, "Really?" I said, "Yes sir," to which he said, "Be at the church the day after tomorrow (Saturday) and you can learn the songs and play with the band on Sunday." I was in big trouble now; I had never ever heard a Christian song before, except maybe Jingle Bells, or Rock around the Christmas tree.

I showed up at the church Saturday and hooked up my 400-watt half stack Ampeg head and short stack. It was powerful. I could have played at Reunion Arena with it; it was overkill. John Hardimon was their worship leader; he was sick as a dog that day. All the songs were charted.

I could not read sheet music, so I wrote down the guitar chords over certain phrases and would just memorize them for tomorrow. It was a nightmare. I should have been fired immediately; it was horrible, but John nicely would send me the music on Monday. I could YouTube it and at least have a sense of what the song was supposed to sound like. Why they let me continue, I will never know.

Thomas and Heather Hoyt, my second and third "Christian friends" who sang on our worship team, would come up to me after playing, saying, "Wow, you did really good today," or "You sounded so good." Great encouragers. I still see both of them weekly, and their characters and natures are still the same.

Simultaneously, with playing on the worship team, reading my Bible, and praying, I also started going to Sunday School, which we did on Wednesday nights. John Hardimon was our teacher and there was about seven to nine of us. As we were getting started (since Catholics don't do Sunday School or read their Bibles, at least none that I ever knew did), I asked the question, "So, how does this work?" John said, "It's a book. Go to page one, read it, and then go to page 2." Genius, I knew I was in the right class. I loved the teaching under John; he knew so much, and it came alive. I am so grateful that God brought into my life the right people. After about two years with Pastor Bill, he got cancer, and the church dispersed. I started going to a church in Mesquite, Texas. We later moved to Royce City, Texas, which is where I did the men's group, the executive pastor thing, and the prayer thing. I was reading a book on prayers by E.M. Bounds, one of the most powerful books ever written on prayer, and was convinced from that book, some of the stories from pastors centuries ago, and their faithfulness in prayer, that we must change things at church. I asked the church's pastor, Pastor Paul, if I could preach a series on prayer. He said absolutely, so after two weeks, this is what I did.

I said, "We all know the power of prayer, so what we are going to do is lock the doors." There was about 120 people in the service that day to pick a day and a time slot within that day and pray. The goal was to pray 24 hours a day, 7 days a week. I would write the "Kingdom prayers" as a starting place. Then each person could pray for what the Holy Spirit wanted them to pray for. Pastor Paul came up to me and said if this works at all for any length of time, we will see the hand of God move mightily. And He did; people started getting saved and then wanted to get baptized. The congregation started to grow; the men's and women's groups started to grow. It was awesome. When you cover a church with that kind of prayer, God hears and moves. Sooner or later, I just think we took our eyes off what was important and there was some different emphasis put on OT teaching, so I left.

The next week, Wendy and I were at Brookhaven church in McKinney, where we both still attend and serve. I teach; Wendy does the children ministry. We love it there and have moved to our new location, new building and academy at Stacy Road, about two miles south of Sam Rayburn Tollway. After several years teaching and serving at Brookhaven, the pastoral staff asked if I would lead a construction ministry for the next year as we built our new building. I got a team together and we would monthly feed the entire construction team 35-80 people at a time. It was a great time to say thank you to the construction team and bless them with the love of Jesus. It was fun and very fulfilling. Once we got into the new building, I was asked to lead a prayer team, I said absolutely, so Pastor Glen preached a series of sermons on prayer. We had signup sheets available. After three weeks or so, we had our team. This was October of 2018; we have about 212 people who pray 7 days a week, 24 hours a day. The results are mind-boggling.

Since I am not on staff, I don't really know all the ins and outs of what goes on at church. I had an appointment with the pastor in January of 2020, and I told him, "I don't know if we are making any difference in this prayer ministry. In fact, I think I am depressed." He asked, "Why do you think you're depressed?" I said, "Well, I watch Gunsmoke and the Hallmark channel every day!!" He them began to share with me some of the stories of what God was doing. He started by prefacing the stories with this; "I have been a pastor for over thirty-six years, and the things are happening have never happened before; it is only because of the prayer ministry and praying God's will."

I will share two of them: The first is about a lady who had emailed him several months earlier. Every morning she left for work and drove down Stacy Road, right past our church. One of the kingdom prayers is that God would draw people to Himself using our church as the conduit. Week after week she drove by, until one day, she drove by, turned around, drove into our parking lot (5:30 am), got out of the car, got on her knees, and asked Jesus to save her. She got saved right there in our parking lot: her, the Holy Spirit, and God the Father, along with Jesus Christ, the savior of mankind.

The second story has to do with the faithfulness of God when you pray His will. Luke 19:10 says, "Jesus came to seek and save that which was lost." It was His kingdom calling\assignment, so does Jesus want people saved? The answer is yes. We know that, so we simply prayed for God to start saving people and that we could see this fruit ...and salvation came, and came, and are still coming, and they are getting baptized afterwards. So, gentlemen, if you have influence in your home church, and you do, start a prayer ministry and hold on. The kingdom will be expanded!!

I had mentioned in chapter 1 that I had got involved with worldwide missions, Here's Life Africa. Andy Blakesly is the president of the organization; it was started by four business guys out of North Carolina, who said there has to more to this Christian life than going to church, teaching Sunday School, and being nice to your wife. This was about twenty-two years ago, around 1999. They have teams of three: they also have a jeep, a projector, and the Jesus film. They go out to the BUSH, show the film, and millions of people have been saved; to date, 22 million + have been saved in about twenty years. You talk about a ministry having a hundred times the fruit; well, here it is. The way the math works is this (2021 numbers), for every .57 you give, someone gets saved. I am in partnership with several worldwide missions and none of them have that amount of return; no one comes close. There are thousands of pastors being raised up to teach all the new converts. Whole tribes are being saved; witch doctors repenting, start taking care of their families biblically. It is just like it was back in Jesus's time.

My Kingdom Assignment: In January of 2017, I again was hooked up with John Hardimon. He had graduated about a year ago with several other high energy marketplace and Christian leaders from a program called "The Master's Program". It takes men who are successful in business and know there is more than just showing up to church every Sunday, taking them through a three-year program to figure what their kingdom assignment is. They met once a quarter (all day) for three years. The program was started about twenty years or so ago by Bob Shank.

We met for lunch. He asked, "George, you are ready to expand your kingdom territory. Come be my guest at the next class." In the beginning, the first two sessions, Bob Shank taught the classes, then the program started to expand rapidly through the United States and now countries overseas are being included, so Bob recruited two graduates, Jeff Gerhart and John Hardimon. In March, I said ok ......my life was about to change forever. The program is very structured, fast paced, and there are recommended "required reading" books. My library has grown by over fifty books (awesome), with precept built on top of precept and culminating with the understanding that we each have a kingdom calling, an assignment of sort. Then the program helps launch you out in your calling, what God designed you for. It is powerful, life-changing, and you will be fulfilled and satisfied with something your life was missing.

It was about halfway through the program, session #6, that I heard the words "kingdom calling" and that even lay people like me had one. I was intrigued. Was there something bigger God wanted me involved in? Several weeks later, I was having lunch with Andy Blakesly from Here's Life Africa. I asked him, "Where is the hardest, most difficult region you guys have?" He thought about it for a minute. "There is one place in Northern Uganda that has unreached people." That means, as far as they know, there are tribes there that have never been introduced to Jesus or the gospel. I said, "That's where I want to be; I wanted to support them with solar Bibles. It has the gospel in their native tongue." The three-man team that shows the Jesus film; I was and am relentless about sharing with people what .57 can do from a kingdom perspective. Remember .57 = 1 salvation!!

I now know what my calling, or assignment, is. It was bigger than what I could ever have imagined, or was it? I was now settling in with my calling, continuing to go to class. We still had another year and half left. Finally, in December of 2020, we had the date to graduate. What started out with a class around twelve to fifteen was now down to three, with one more doing a ZOOM graduation. Two weeks before graduation, the teachers, Jeff and John, got together with the future graduates to go over all of our assessment tests and talk/question, us to make sure we figured out what we were created for.

By now we all knew scripturally that we were created for a calling, an assignment. They were there to help launch us out.

As we talked, I told them that at every chance I had while teaching Sunday school, I would point out, biblically, people who had their callings. Examples: Moses set my people free; David was the king of Israel; John the Baptist was the ambassador of Jesus, and Jesus Himself left the glory of heaven, lived completely as a man, got beaten up, and die for all the sins of mankind. And then because He completed His assignment, His Father raised Him from the dead on the third day. He now sits at the Father's right hand, a place of power and pre menace. By the time we were through talking, they both looked at me, were smiling, and said, "George, don't you see it?" I said, "See what?" "Your kingdom calling? Your kingdom calling, your assignment, is to tell people, to teach people, that they have a calling on their lives. You are so passionate with this assignment; it is effortless as you teach it. It is what you were designed to do" ... they were right!

I will continue to be involved in Here's Life Africa, with that calling, but I can't wait to see the fruit from this calling. You were created for a calling, for an assignment.

You can't deny it after all the scriptural evidence. Start asking God what it is, and He will show you. Remember, you are a kingdom-created person, and eternity is waiting for all of us. The words will come: "Well done good and faithful servant, come and enter into the joy of YOUR Lord."

Chapter 8

FIRST THINGS FIRST.....
HAVE YOU ASKED
FOR THE GIFT?

In the Gospel of John, chapter 3, a Pharisee (religious leader who knew the Old Testament and taught in the Synagogues) named Nicodemus has an encounter with Jesus. During the conversation Jesus tells him that to see the Kingdom of God one must be born again. Nicodemus ask, can one enter his mother's womb a second time, and then be born again?

Nicodemus was thinking "earthly birth ", Jesus was talking about a spiritual birth. In Romans chapter 3 the Apostle Paul says this vs 10-12, **As it is written:**

"There is none righteous, no not one. There is none who understands. There is none who seeks after God. They have all turned aside; They have together become unprofitable; There is none who do good, no, not one." You see God is Holy (He is set apart, there is no sin in Him, He is above reproach, He is Transcendent, Majestic, Eternal, Omnipresent, Perfect, Sovereign, Good, Mighty, Knows everything).

So, what are we to do? Romans 3 :23 says, **"for all have sinned and fall short of the Glory of God."**
You see, we all have sinned (committed an immoral act that is a transgression against God's divine law). Sin separates us from God, and we all have sinned, and do sin. There is nothing we can do to make ourselves "clean" before a Holy God, nothing. But you see you don't have to. God through His son Jesus has made a way to be with God. It happened at the cross. Jesus left the majesty of His Father in heaven and was born here on earth. He was fully man, and fully God at the same

time (I don't understand everything in that part of the sentence either, I just believe, because the bible says it), (John 1:1,3,14,17,18, **"but the gift of God is eternal life in Christ Jesus or Lord"**. He lived a sinless life in thought, words, actions .... HE was PERFECT. So, what did He do, He became a sacrifice for us, why **"because the wage of sin is death"**, Romans 6:23.

You see there is a penalty for sin, and it is death, complete removal from the presence of God. There is a place for people when they do not know God, it is hell, a place of torment, anguish, torture, fire, and it lasts forever, you will never escape FOREVER.

So, if the penalty of sin is death, Jesus, the son of God, said, I will go in "their" (yours and mine) place and die for them. So, Jesus went willingly to be tortured, beaten, and ridiculed for you and me, they crucified Him. In John chapter 19:30 Jesus cries out "it is finished ". What did He mean? It means there is nothing more that mankind (you and me) can or have to do to be "right "with God. God offers the gift of salvation to all. It is a gift, you don' t has to do anything but receive it.

Above all, God LOVES YOU! He always has. Romans chapter 10, vs. 9,10 says **"that if you confess**

with your mouth the Lord Jesus and believe in your heart that God has raised Him from the dead, you will be saved. For with the heart one believes unto righteousness, and with the mouth confession is made unto salvation."

So, do you want to know God, do you want to have your sins forgiven, past, present and future? You can.

Pray with me, you can say something like this, it's not the words that save you, it the "heart "behind the words!

Lord, I have sinned, I have no power with in me not to sin, but I am sorry, I don't completely understand salvation and sin completely, but I don't have to, I now put my trust in you. I want you to forgive me, I want to be born again. I turn my life over to you. thank you for loving me and saving me, in Jesus' name I pray these things, AMEN.

Congratulations, I am so proud of you, God has "good works "that He created before the creation of the world, ask God what your Kingdom calling is, and may the favor and hand of God be with you, may he reveal Himself to you un a special unique way .... hang on, the Kingdom of God is fixing to be expanded earthly and eternity. I will see you in heaven and you can tell me what your Kingdom calling was. Get ready to hear these words.......

"Well done my good and faithful servant."

Recommended reading and ministries:

Life Mastery
by Bob Shank

The Treasure Principle
by Randy Alcorn

Gospel Patrons
by John Rinehart

The Kingdom Assignment
by Denny and Leesa Bellesi

The Master's Program
(https://www.mastersprogram.org/summary.pdf)

Here's Life Africa
(https://hereslifeafrica.com)

ENDNOTES

1 Merriam-Webster Dictionary, online (2021), s.v. "calling."

2 Strong's Exhaustive Concordance, viewed online on BibleHub.com., s.v. "yatsar" (3335), accessed May 5, 2021, https://biblehub.com/strongs/d.htm.

3 Strong's Exhaustive Concordance, viewed online on BibleHub.com, s.v. "radah" (7287), accessed May 5, 2021, https://biblehub.com/strongs/h.htm.

4 Merriam-Webster Dictionary, online (2021), s.v. "blessed."

5 Merriam-Webster Dictionary, online (2021), s.v. "chosen."

6 Merriam-Webster Dictionary, online, (2021), s.v. "predestined."

7 Merriam-Webster Dictionary, online, (2021), s.v. "adopt."

8 Merriam-Webster Dictionary, online, (2021), s.v. "accept."

9 Merriam-Webster Dictionary, online, (2021), s.v. "redeem."

10 Merriam-Webster Dictionary, online, (2021), s.v. "forgiveness."

11 Merriam-Webster Dictionary, online, (2021), s.v. "enlightened."

12 Merriam-Webster Dictionary, online, (2021), s.v. "inheritance."

13 Merriam-Webster Dictionary, online, (2021), s.v. "seal."

14 Merriam-Webster Dictionary, online, (2021), s.v. "assured."

15 Merriam-Webster Dictionary, online, (2021), s.v. "ownership."

16 Merriam-Webster Dictionary, online, (2021), s.v. "stewardship."

17 Merriam-Webster Dictionary, online, (2021), s.v. "purpose."

18 Merriam-Webster Dictionary, online, (2021), s.v. "passion."

9 781662 823008